# The CQ Press Career Guide for Political Science Students

# The CQ Press Career Guide for Political Science Students

**Wendy N. Whitman Cobb**
*Cameron University*

FOR INFORMATION:

CQ Press

An Imprint of SAGE Publications, Inc.

2455 Teller Road

Thousand Oaks, California 91320

E-mail: order@sagepub.com

SAGE Publications Ltd.

1 Oliver's Yard

55 City Road

London EC1Y 1SP

United Kingdom

SAGE Publications India Pvt. Ltd.

B 1/I 1 Mohan Cooperative Industrial Area

Mathura Road, New Delhi 110 044

India

SAGE Publications Asia-Pacific Pte. Ltd.

3 Church Street

#10-04 Samsung Hub

Singapore 049483

Printed in the United States of America

Library of Congress Cataloging-in-Publication Data

Names: Whitman-Cobb, Wendy N. Whitman, author.

Title: The CQ Press career guide for political science students / Wendy N. Whitman-Cobb.

Other titles: Congressional Quarterly Press career guide for political science students

Description: Washington, D.C. : CQ Press, 2018. | Includes index.

Identifiers: LCCN 2017014866 | ISBN 9781506386911 (alk. paper)

Subjects: LCSH: Political science—Vocational guidance—United States. | Vocational guidance—United States.

Classification: LCC JA88.U6 W46 2018 | DDC 320.023/73—dc23
LC record available at https://lccn.loc.gov/2017014866

This book is printed on acid-free paper.

Acquisitions Editor:  Matt Byrnie

Editorial Assistant:  Zachary Hoskins

Production Editor:  Kimaya Khashnobish

Copy Editor:  Jared Leighton

Typesetter:  C&M Digitals (P) Ltd.

Proofreader:  Sue Irwin

Indexer:  Diggs Publication Services

Cover Designer:  Anupama Krishnan

Marketing Manager:  Amy Whitaker

MIX
Paper from responsible sources
FSC® C012947

17 18 19 20 21 10 9 8 7 6 5 4 3 2 1

# Contents

**Preface**     **vii**

**Chapter 1: Careers in Political Science**     **1**
Government Careers     1
Private-Sector Jobs     6
Academics     12

**Chapter 2: Political Science as a Degree**     **15**
Planning Your College Career     17
Conclusion     24

**Chapter 3: Acing the Interview**     **25**
Looking for a Job     25
Preparing an Application     29
The Interview     37

**Chapter 4: Choosing a Graduate School**     **41**
Law School     41
Graduate School     45

**Index**     **49**
**About the Author**     **51**

# Preface

## Introduction

As a professor, one of the duties that I spend much of my time on is advising students who are either majoring in political science or thinking about it. One of the very first questions I ask these students is, What do you want to do after college? Often, my students are unsure about what they want to do and, in some cases, don't even know what they can do with a political science degree. What they do know, though, is that they find politics interesting and want to spend more time learning about it.

When I became a political science major as an undergraduate, I didn't even know what I was going to do after college. In fact, political science wasn't even my first major; I spent the first six weeks of my college life as a theatre major until I realized that I simply lacked the drive and ambition of my theatre peers to succeed. Thankfully, I was taking an American government class at the time, and based on my lifelong interest in politics and current events, I decided to make the leap. I am glad every day that I did because today, I get to study things that I am passionate about and spend my days with students who are every bit as excited as I am.

This book is intended to answer some of the questions that my students have had over the years about careers in political science. These include the different career fields that political science majors can pursue and just how they go about getting there. To that end, it is important to note that not even this book covers absolutely everything that political science majors have gone on to do. Political science majors have become athletes, journalists, award-winning writers, researchers, musicians, and, yes, elected officials, including presidents. The reason that a political science degree nets entry into such wide and varied fields is because of the range of information and skills that are imparted to you by your professors. Critical thinking, reading, writing, debate, research, and statistics are just some of the very important life skills that you will find helpful inside—and especially outside—of the classroom.

## Why I Became a Political Scientist

While not every experience is typical, I can speak for myself in saying that political science has allowed me to study things that I find interesting and exciting.

Growing up in Florida, one of the most exciting things you once got to see were space shuttle launches originating from Kennedy Space Center. I always found the launches fascinating, especially those in the middle of the night. When I arrived as an undergraduate at the University of Central Florida, I found that they offered classes in both space history and space policy, opportunities that I quickly availed myself of. I had never been adept at math or science, so becoming an astronaut was not on my career radar. However, I quickly discovered that by using the tools of political science, I could research and learn about space. I have not looked back since.

As I moved toward finishing my undergraduate degree, at some point along the way, I decided that I would become an academic political scientist, someone working as a college professor, teaching, researching, and writing. I pursued a master's degree in political science, also at UCF, before moving onto the University of Florida for a PhD. Throughout, my research focused heavily on space policy and space issues, and I found myself bringing together streams of knowledge from throughout political science. I took classes not only in American politics and policy but also public administration and comparative politics. This broad education has served me well, allowing me to teach multiple areas as I have entered my own career.

After I finished my PhD, I was lucky enough to find a job as an assistant professor at Cameron University in Lawton, Oklahoma. Cameron is a small regional state school, but this has given me the opportunity to work closely with my students and know them on a personal basis. In my position, I teach a wide range of classes, from American government, the class I first got my start in, to research methods, international studies, and even zombies and politics. I continue to pursue research in areas I find interesting, including cancer policy and science and technology policy in general. I coach our Model United Nations team and serve on the board of the Midwest Model United Nations organization. In short, I get to spend my days learning new things and relaying them to some pretty amazing students.

## Plan of the Book

As I stated before, this book is partially based on the questions I get from my students and what they want to know to succeed. To that end, the first chapter lays out many career opportunities that can be open to political science majors, both inside and outside of government. Chapter 2 then provides some ideas about the types of classes and extracurricular activities that you may want to consider based on the career path you would like to follow. Chapter 3 provides some of the tricks of the trade that I and many others have picked up for applying to jobs, preparing applications, and successfully interviewing for positions. Finally, Chapter 4 lays out the path to both law school and graduate school, including questions that you will want to consider as you choose your next direction.

## Acknowledgments

This book has been deeply influenced by my experiences working with students. I thank all of my students heartily for giving me ideas and suggestions to cover in this short guide. I also wish to thank the editors at SAGE/CQ Press for the opportunity to write this piece. Finally, thank you to my husband and all of my family for continually supporting me as I became the political scientist I am today. As always, any errors or omissions remain solely my own.

# Chapter 1

# Careers in Political Science

When we think of jobs you can get with a degree in political science, we typically think of things like a politician, lawyer, or maybe a teacher. While this is the case, there are many more professions and career paths available than the ones you've probably thought of before. The key reason this is the case is because of the wide variety of skills that you learn as a political science major. Research, writing, teamwork, critical thinking and analysis, critical reading, debate, and argumentation skills can all be parlayed into valuable career fields that will have you living on your own in no time.

The purpose of this chapter is to explore the types of career paths, both public and private, that you can pursue with a degree in political science. While this won't be a complete guide to everything you can do, we hope to give you some resources and ideas for further education. We'll start off with the more obvious careers, such as those that will take you to the halls of government, and then move into the private sector, where jobs can be had in everything from business and finance to administration, the media, and non-profits. Finally, we'll discuss the academic path that can take you (back) into the classroom.

## Government Careers

When talking about careers in government, the typical ones come to mind: a politician, a staff member for an elected official, or some sort of administrative job. But there are so many more opportunities available in the government and not only the federal government. Although the federal government employs over 2.5 million people (not including the military), state and local governments employ almost 16 million more people! In looking just at the federal government, a good way to think about the job opportunities available is from the top down.

## Working for Elected Officials

Elected officials can't do it alone. They rely on a small army of staff members to support their activities and foster relationships with constituents and other politicians. Every member of Congress is allocated a budget with which to build their office and attract personnel, allowing them to decide how many staffers to hire and for what functions. You could be an advisor on specific policy areas or a communications aide, assisting members of Congress with outreach to the public, the media, and their constituents. You will also assist members with researching and creating legislation, negotiating with other members of Congress, and being a liaison with committees and their work.

On the home front, members of Congress create offices in their districts and states to facilitate contact with their voters. Part of the work of these staff members is something called constituent service. Whenever you are having a problem with some area of government, be it Social Security, immigration, or the military, you can contact your member of Congress, and he or she will attempt to intercede on your behalf. This valuable function not only assists voters with their everyday problems but makes it more likely that they will vote for that congressman or woman in future elections. This is just another task you could be hired to do when working for members of Congress.

Outside of members' offices, Congress requires a multitude of others to get their work done. Staff members are hired for individual committees, and party organizations also hire staff. For example, the Judiciary Committee in either the House or the Senate hires people whose sole job is to work on issues related to that committee. Both the Democratic and Republican caucuses and their respective campaign committees also hire staff to coordinate activities among their members. These types of jobs require good communications skills, the ability to process and understand political issues, and the ability to work together as part of a team. Although many of these jobs come with hard work and long hours, you'll have the opportunity to see the political and legislative process up close and personal.

Congress also has nonpartisan organizations that assist members in getting their work done. The Congressional Budget Office (CBO) and the Government Accountability Office (GAO) are two such agencies. The CBO provides independent, nonpartisan budgetary information to members to help them in the annual budgetary process. It provides estimates of annual revenue and program costs and calculates the official cost of pending legislation. The GAO performs investigations into the performance and activities of executive branch agencies. Members of Congress can request that the GAO investigate certain policies, programs, or organizations and the GAO will report back its findings to the member and the rest of Congress.

These organizations provide several job opportunities for political science majors who are interested in the nuts and bolts of budgetary and government policy and can be effective in their ability to communicate.

Job opportunities also abound in the White House, where you can work on domestic policy, communications, outreach and the media, working with the Congress, and so much more. While we normally only see a few select top advisors on TV representing the president, there are hundreds more individuals working in the West Wing organizing everything the White House and the president do. The White House also contains agencies like the Office of Management and Budget, which assists the president in constructing his or her annual budget. Like the Congress, White House staffers are likely to spend long hours at the office, but it doesn't hurt that the office is the White House.

Don't forget about the elected officials at the state and local level. Members of state legislative bodies in all fifty states require the help of others to complete the job they were elected for, and many of the same responsibilities that members of Congress give to their staff members are also reflected in state legislatures. This means that by working for a state legislator, you have the opportunity to contribute to issues that are likely to be important to your fellow citizens and have a far more immediate impact. For example, the state of California has an economy that rivals some of the largest economies around the world; the immediacy of monetary policy and government spending makes it so that the actions of state legislators are likely to impact Californians quite directly. State governors also require a large amount of assistance in formulating policies and carrying them out. Since state governments carry out most of the day-to-day activities of governing, these types of jobs can have a very real impact on your community and state.

## The Military

Political science degrees can also lead to excellent careers in the U.S. military. In order to be an officer in most branches of the armed forces, you must hold a bachelor's degree, and although the military does not specify what that degree must be in, political science provides future military officers with the knowledge of world affairs and domestic politics that help sharpen their analytical skills.

As the Prussian military theorist Carl von Clausewitz wrote, "War is the continuation of politics by other means." The military is ultimately a tool of foreign policy that is placed under the control of a civilian, elected leadership. Being able to understand not only the history of international affairs and its effect on military doctrine but current events is crucial to understanding the role the military plays and what it's capable of doing. For example, an understanding of the rise of the Islamic State in the Middle East can be important but so is understanding how other militaries have fought terrorist insurgents. This is part of the reason that military history is often a required class for ROTC cadets in college.

Sometimes, in the course of duty, troops will be asked to work with soldiers from other states, the United Nations, or NATO. Often, international soldiers come to American military schools for additional training, and this is a tool for furthering relations with those states. Cooperating with individual soldiers from other places may be easy, but often, dealing with the foreign military machinery may be hard. An understanding of those countries and their geopolitical situations will ease those situations and further American military and diplomatic goals.

## The Bureaucracy

Not only are there fifteen major cabinet departments in the federal government, but there are countless smaller agencies and offices that deal with everything from getting Social Security checks out on time to regulating the stock market. If there is something you're interested in, chances are there's a bureaucracy that's involved in that policy area. You can be a federal agent with the FBI; the Bureau of Alcohol, Tobacco, Firearms and Explosives; or the Drug Enforcement Agency. You can be in the diplomatic corps of the Department of State or a doctor in Veterans Affairs. While many of these jobs may require more specialized education, there are any numbers of interesting jobs available.

The first stop when looking for a job with the federal government is the website USAJobs.gov, which provides an updated list of positions available and maintains an application system you would use to apply for those positions. (USA Jobs will be covered in further detail in Chapter 3.) USA Jobs provides a quick reference list of jobs available by major in college, and while political science does appear on the list, there are a number of other related career paths you can also consider:

- Business or commercial law
- Community planning/development
- Economics
- Global public policy
- History

- International trade, finance
- International relations
- Humanities
- Administration
- Statistics
- Urban planning

What is intriguing about many of these positions is that you don't have to live in Washington, D.C., to pursue a career in the federal bureaucracy. Many agencies have offices located throughout the United States at which you can find appointments. Larger communities will often have Social Security offices, or if you live near a military post, you can find jobs on base or with the VA.

One line of bureaucratic work that you may find interesting is that of regulatory work. Examples of regulatory agencies include the Securities and Exchange Committee (SEC), which oversees banks and the stock market; the Environmental Protection Agency (EPA), which regulates environmental issues; the Food and Drug Administration (FDA), whose responsibilities include approving prescription drugs and overseeing food preparation and labeling; and the Federal Aviation Administration (FAA), which regulates airports and airlines. The main purpose of regulatory agencies is to take the laws that have been passed by Congress and turn them into actual workable rules that industry must follow. Not only do regulators write these rules, but it's also up to them to investigate compliance with and enforcement of them.

Another example of interesting and exciting work can be found in the U.S. Foreign Service. The Foreign Service comprises the diplomats carrying out U.S. foreign and diplomatic policy around the world. An understanding of languages, cultures, and customs is requisite, but being a Foreign Service officer provides you with the opportunity to travel throughout the world and be stationed at one of hundreds of embassies or consulates, actively contributing to the mission of the United States at home and abroad. You can specialize in a functional area, like politics or economics, or in a geographical area, depending on your experience and education. Becoming a Foreign Service officer is a demanding and rigorous process, with the Department of State looking for those individuals who possess a wide array of knowledge and significant international experience. While there is no specific educational requirement to become a Foreign Service officer, a degree in political science can provide the political and economic background that is often tested in the Foreign Service Exam. Participation can lead to a fulfilling career, with the top echelons of the Foreign Service often serving important and high-placed diplomatic roles throughout the world.

Jobs in the bureaucracy, especially in the federal civil service, provide lots of room for career advancement. Once in, you can compete for higher pay and promotions, and if positions are available, you have the option of moving to different areas. Although bureaucrats are often maligned, these types of jobs are necessary for the everyday functioning of American government. It might seem boring, but the jobs these bureaucrats are carrying out can be exciting and rewarding.

## Peace Corps

Established by President John F. Kennedy in 1961, the Peace Corps is an esteemed volunteer program that provides needed assistance throughout the world in areas ranging from health and agriculture to economic development. With almost seven thousand volunteers serving worldwide, the Peace Corps is an attractive postcollege option but can be quite competitive to get into. There is no general application for the Peace Corps; instead, potential volunteers apply for specific positions in designated countries. This allows potential volunteers to choose which projects interest them the most and which projects they can most directly benefit. Most volunteers serve in a two-year program, but quick-response teams are also open to past volunteers. A political science degree can provide excellent preparation for a stint in the corps, as understanding global dynamics, institutions, and development are key when participating in Peace Corps projects.

### Lawyers

One profession often crosses the boundary between public and private: the law. Not only can you practice in private, lawyers are in demand in the public sector. While being a lawyer in court is what usually comes to mind when you think about the law, there are plenty of other positions for lawyers in the government. Lawyers can be used when crafting and creating legislation, when analyzing legal implications for policy, and for interpreting and implementing legislation.

The most obvious place for lawyers in government is the Department of Justice, which is responsible for investigating and prosecuting federal crimes. However, most bureaucracies have legal departments whose responsibilities include analyzing legislation, writing regulations, ensuring that all laws are being followed, and recommending policy directives. Lawyers also have a role to play in the Department of Defense, as they can provide guidance on the interpretation of international agreements like the Geneva Convention. Similarly, lawyers are instrumental in crafting diplomatic agreements and treaties, centered in the Department of State.

One area of law that is particularly important for the bureaucracy is called administrative law. Administrative law involves the body of law that governs how the government is organized and run. Administrative law includes things like regulations that bureaucracies craft and administer and how those regulations are carried out. The major piece of legislation that governs administrative law is the Administrative Procedures Act of 1946. The APA requires that bureaucracies wishing to publish new regulations must follow certain procedures to not only inform the public of those regulations but to give the public an opportunity to comment on them before they are put into effect. Many challenges to regulations today come out of the APA and the requirements it lays out for making and implementing regulations. In fact, this is so consequential that there is an entire court system, the administrative courts, that hears cases related to administrative law.

## Private-Sector Jobs

By the term *private sector*, we mean nongovernment jobs. Believe it or not, as many job opportunities that exist in the government for political science majors, there are even more in the private sector. Since we left off talking about lawyers in government service, we'll pick up with that topic here.

### Lawyers

If you watch much television, you're probably quite familiar with the sight of the courtroom lawyers. They either work for government to prosecute crimes or are defense attorneys, defending their clients from a charge or set of charges. While this is certainly a legitimate area of law, there are far more other areas of law that you could become interested in if you choose to become a lawyer. Here's just a sampling:

| | | |
|---|---|---|
| — Animal law | — Constitutional law | — Juvenile law |
| — Antitrust law | — Contract law | — Marital law |
| — Banking law | — Entertainment law | — Music law |
| — Business law | — Family law | — Patent law |
| — Communications law | — Health law | — Space law |
| | — Immigration law | — Sports law |

Law degrees can also lead to jobs in entertainment or sports as an agent or representative for business affairs or contracts. It can also be parlayed into teaching constitutional law or writing on judicial issues for the media. Just because you get a law degree does not mean you're limited in the types of things you can do with it.

## Campaigns and Elections

Just as there are opportunities for lawyers both in and out of government service, jobs in the realm of campaigns and elections straddle the border as well. Due to laws restricting the use of governmental staff in the service of campaigning, when politicians run for office, they require a whole separate apparatus to organize and run their campaigns. Opportunities to work on political campaigns are wide and varied but unfortunately ebb and flow with the coming and going of election season. Campaign operatives are needed to assist in organizing travel for both the candidate and needed staffers, communicating with the press, establishing a message to potential voters, mobilizing potential voters, writing speeches, testing public opinion, and, perhaps most importantly, raising money. Today's modern campaigns require staffers to address new dimensions of life and society, including social media and rapid reaction to comments made by others. Often, jobs with candidates can be parlayed into government positions, if and when the favored candidate wins election.

The importance and scale of campaigns and elections are such that cottage industries specializing in all of these tasks have grown to behemoth scale. These policy shops provide specialized advice to candidates and their campaigns about what their message should be or sound like, the appearance of the candidates themselves, public policy issues, and public opinion. In fact, pollsters, those who construct and conduct public opinion polls, are in high demand not just for those seeking public office but those already in it. Other firms provide services such as crafting media messages and campaign commercials. One of the most important services that these operatives can offer is on how to raise the enormous amounts of money that are often needed to run successful campaigns. A political science degree is excellent preparation for these professions because, in addition to the basic knowledge gained, many programs require courses in research methods and statistical methods that impart strong analytical research skills.

One final area of employment in the arena of campaigns and elections is that of campaign finance law. Given the flow of money into politics today and the complicated laws and regulations about what can and cannot be accepted, campaign finance lawyers are often needed to advise campaigns on what is acceptable or not and to file the required disclosures that most all candidates must file revealing who has given what to their campaign. These lawyers can play powerful roles in the outcomes of elections themselves not only by advising candidates but by shaping the interpretation of campaign finance law.

## Business and Finance

Political science degrees can also lead to promising positions in business settings, particularly businesses that have interactions with governments, domestic or foreign. Think about what you learn as a political science major. Your knowledge of global affairs, international organizations, and international politics can assist major global corporations in navigating international hurdles when foreign governments must be considered or dealt with. Many large businesses and financial institutions undoubtedly have foreign dealings, particularly in countries with favorable tax laws.

One of the areas in which political science degrees can be useful is in global trade. The recent negotiation and signing of the Trans-Pacific Partnership is a work not only in politics but economics and trade. It takes quick thinking and a solid foundation of knowledge to be able to negotiate issues not only between countries but between businesses and states. If this line of work sounds interesting, you may wish to consider a minor in business or economics along with a political science major (or admittedly, vice versa).

Businesses often require expertise in the areas of administration and evaluation. An education in the fields of public policy and/or public administration can provide a potential employer with a way to understand their business from a cultural or institutional perspective. Experts in public administration not only help in the everyday functioning of the organization but provide advice on how organizations should be structured or reformed to make them more efficient and effective.

Policy evaluation, or the analyzing of outcomes and outputs of policy to determine if and how well they are solving the intended problems, can help industry understand their own policy initiatives and ensure that they are implemented in a sensible fashion. Any time a company institutes a new policy, the skills of a good evaluator can be used. Program and policy evaluators are often hired on by a company to perform in-house evaluations of their operations and provide policy advice. While evaluators can also form their own operation that can then be contracted to perform evaluations, they are equally as likely to be hired to be on staff.

## Nonprofits, Nongovernmental Organizations, and Foundations

Interest groups are those organizations which seek to influence public policy in ways other than getting candidates elected. Examples of these include the National Rifle Association (NRA), People for the Ethical Treatment of Animals (PETA), the National Association for the Advancement of Colored People (NAACP), or the American Civil Liberties Union (ACLU). These organizations are only the beginning of the different types of organizations you can work for with a political science degree—interest groups, nongovernmental organizations (NGOs), political action committees (PACs) and super PACs, charity foundations, and other nonprofit organizations can benefit from your knowledge.

For interest groups, in particular, you could go to work as a lobbyist working to influence government on that group's issues. Lobbyists work to persuade government officials to support and pursue an interest group's desired policy direction. They are involved in shaping public thought on major issues and proposing policy solutions and can be intricately involved in crafting legislation. In joining an interest group, you can also provide advice on the direction of their public campaigns and informing the public without necessarily becoming a lobbyist. There are thousands of interest groups out there, so chances are you can find a group that aligns with issues you're interested in, from animal welfare to salt and sugar in processed foods to veterans' issues.

If you are interested in lobbying government, there are also firms in Washington, D.C., and in state capitols across the country whose only job is lobbying. Other organizations will pay money to the lobbying firm to represent their interests in Washington. As a lobbyist working for one of these firms, you would likely be representing a handful or interests and organizations not only to lawmakers but also as a communicator alerting your clients to issues going on that might affect them.

PACs and super PACs are organizations that represent groups or individuals and raise money on behalf of an issue or a candidate. Working for one of these groups would bring you into contact with electioneering activities like raising money, crafting a message, creating a public relations plan, and campaigning on behalf of your topic or candidate. In recent election cycles, the role of super PACs has only been growing, and some have raised millions of dollars on behalf of their issues and candidates. In fact, you could even create your own super PAC with a relatively small amount of time and effort. The same is true of interest groups!

Nongovernmental organizations are nonprofit citizen groups that can be organized locally, nationally, or internationally. Some examples of these include the American Red Cross and the International Red Cross, Doctors Without Borders, CARE International, and Greenpeace. These types of organizations provide services that governments either cannot or would not provide or advocate for specific issues; for example, Doctors Without Borders was instrumental in fighting the recent Ebola outbreak in West Africa. Because these organizations often work with governments and international organizations like the United Nations, knowledge of governmental affairs is requisite for the easy functioning of these organizations.

## Think Tanks

A relatively new type of organization has also become influential in politics: think tanks. Think tanks are organizations that hire teams of people to research and write in particular areas of policy. Think tanks have become significant in some policy circles because of their thorough research reports on current policy issues. The proposals they put forward are often adopted by politicians who then integrate them into legislation. Given that the focus of think tanks is on current policy problems, think tanks may be an ideal profession for the political science major who enjoys research and writing.

Typically, think tanks will focus on a particular policy area and prepare written reports on what the government is doing or not doing or what the think tank believes the government should be doing. In addition, they craft policy documents that they hope to use to influence policymakers and thought leaders. Other think tanks are organized around particular ideologies. The Heritage Foundation is a conservative think tank; they tackle multiple policy areas but from a conservative, Republican angle. On the liberal side of the spectrum, the Center for American Progress uses the motto "Progressive ideas for a strong, just, and free America." Of course, there are any number of think tanks that are nonpartisan or nonideological, like the Brookings Institution, the Carter Institute, Freedom House, or RAND.

## Media

The media is a fantastic outlet for work in political science. Many political science graduates have turned their degrees into careers in journalism precisely because they understand the intricacies of government and how the system operates. In addition to the major news outlets that you can think of, there are some news-gathering operations that exist solely to track the comings and goings in the political world. Some of these include *Politico* and *Congressional Quarterly*. Most large news organizations will have Washington bureaus to cover and report on the federal government. Local news channels and newspapers will often find the occurrences of their state and local governments as front page news. Additionally, the skills you develop in researching and writing as a political science major will add to your appeal.

Today, the media doesn't just consist of the radio, newspaper, and television outlets. Social media has thrown open the doors to different types of media and journalists. Twitter has a handle dedicated specifically to government in the U.S. and across the world. Facebook has become a major source of political information, for better or for worse. Blogs and independent reporting also have a major impact;

for example Erick Erickson, a conservative commentator, made his mark with the blog and news site redstate.com. While news coverage on the *Huffington Post* has broadened into pop culture and entertainment, the website started by Arianna Huffington started out as a liberal news site. The openness of the Internet has not only revolutionized the media but has allowed independent journalists to make a mark on their profession.

In addition to becoming a journalist, you could also go to work as a communications advisor for politicians, parties, or other organizations. Particularly with the growth of social media, the ability for people and organizations to be able to communicate effectively with citizens has become even more important. Politicians find they must monitor feeds on Twitter and Facebook to get a good feel of the public pulse. New social media sites are popping up all the time, and young people are in the perfect place to understand not only their usefulness but how to use them to their fullest advantage. Combined with knowledge of politics, you can make yourself an attractive job candidate.

## Teaching

Unfortunately, teaching is an undervalued field; state requirements are steep, parents are demanding, and students are often difficult. Despite this, teaching the next generation of citizens is a rewarding and fulfilling career option. While teaching at the college level will be taken up shortly, teaching in middle and high schools is another option for those with a political science degree. These formative years are important for imparting a basic knowledge of government to children and to stoke interest in political affairs. High school civics and government courses are often required of all students, and a good teacher can prepare his or her students for citizenship by being an effective communicator, as well as being knowledgeable about her or his subject area.

Many educators find their way to teaching through an education degree; however, you can still enter the field without it. Some universities offer an education or educational studies minor; pairing that with a political science degree will give you not only needed knowledge in politics but also prepare you for the rigors of the classroom, including lessons plans, classroom management, and assessment. Depending on the state in which you plan to teach, there may be alternative-certification programs, where those without an education background take classes and exams that will certify them to teach after they have already gotten into the classroom. Additionally, you may enter the teaching profession and then decide to pursue a graduate degree in education.

If you are interested in a career in education and either wish to serve in underperforming communities or are perhaps unsure about it long term, you can participate in a national program called Teach for America. Upon being accepted into the program, you will be hired by a school in an underperforming area for two years throughout which Teach for America will provide you training in education and teaching. By participating, you will not only gain valuable experience but you will be putting your education to good use by educating the next generation in some of the areas around the country that are most desperate for good teachers. Additionally, the experience will bolster your résumé for employers and other professional and graduate programs you may wish to enter.

## Academics

Once you have achieved an undergraduate degree in political science, you may begin to think about furthering that education and perhaps eventually becoming a university professor or academic. This means you not only conduct your own research into and about politics but you also teach at a university, college, or community college. Within academia, there are different activities you can undertake that require different degrees. The best way to explore these is to discuss what you can do in academia with what degree you achieve. A bachelor's degree would be what you pursue as an undergraduate. Although you could use that to become a teacher in K–12, you'll need an advanced degree to work at the college level.

The next level is a master's, and it usually requires between thirty and forty hours of graduate credit, depending on the institution. These classes provide you with more in-depth knowledge of political science and the research that has already been completed in the field. You will be asked to select a concentration where you will focus your studies. Some degrees require the completion of qualifying exams, a thesis, or both. Qualifying exams or comprehensive exams vary depending on your school, but in general, they consist of a set of questions you will be asked to answer either in written form, orally, or both. A thesis is an independent research project you will undertake under the guidance of a faculty advisor and faculty committee. The length will vary, but it will generally contain a number of chapters and extensive independent research.

The completion of an MA in political science allows you to teach at the college level. The classes you are qualified to teach often depend on the concentration you selected. If you selected international relations as your field of study, you'll be better qualified to teach classes in that area than you will be in political theory. While instructors with MAs find jobs at community colleges, junior colleges, and state universities, most faculty positions require even more education.

A PhD in political science amplifies the requirements of the MA. Depending on your school, you'll need somewhere around ninety hours of graduate course work, inclusive of dissertation credit hours. At this point, you'll need to pick your major field of concentration and one or two minor fields. These fields should be selected depending on what you find most interesting since, after all, you'll be spending many years studying this. Like the MA, you'll also be asked to take qualifying exams before you are admitted to PhD candidacy. PhD candidacy means you have completed all of the requirements for a PhD except for a dissertation. (This status is also known as ABD, or "all but dissertation.") A dissertation is a book-length work of individual research, again conducted under the supervision of a committee of faculty headed by your main dissertation advisor.

A dissertation is usually what takes the longest to complete; some PhD candidates take upwards of three to four years to complete it! This does not mean it *will* take that long, however. It often takes that long because brand-new research projects take time to establish, and assembling data and research takes even longer. On average, PhD candidates complete their dissertation in two years' time. Once your dissertation is complete, you will be subjected to an academic ritual called the defense. In front of your committee (and others, if invited), you will have to defend your work. If your advisor is smart, he or she will not let you defend until you are ready, but sometimes, defenses can be difficult. Only once you successfully defend your dissertation are you granted the PhD.

A PhD, as the terminal degree in political science, allows you to teach at colleges and universities. There are two types of job tracks in academia, tenure track and non–tenure track. Non–tenure track jobs will not confer tenure (essentially a long-term, guaranteed contract for your job), nor will they allow much room for promotion. However, the requirements to perform research will be much less or nonexistent. In other words, non–tenure track positions are usually focused solely on the teaching of undergraduates and, in some cases, graduate students. A tenure track position allows you entrance into the hierarchy of professors. The entry-level professor is what's called an assistant professor, and she or he is non-tenured. Depending on the school you work at, you will not only teach but perform significant amounts of research and school service. On average, after five to six years, you are reviewed by the faculty at your school and considered for tenure and promotion to the rank of associate professor. Again, after five to six years of continued teaching, research, and service, you can be promoted to the top rank, a full professor.

The bottom line to any university, tenure track job is that you will be performing multiple tasks in addition to teaching. You will need to publish research articles in peer-reviewed academic journals or even books. Additionally, you will be expected to provide service in your school and your discipline. This can take the form of serving on faculty committees or working within your own department advising student groups or providing career services. Service in the discipline can include serving as a peer reviewer for a journal or for textbooks or serving as a discussant or chair at conferences.

Once in academia, professors often have the option of moving into administration. Administration includes all of those people who are responsible for running the school: the department chairs, deans, provosts, and even the school presidents. Sometimes, these positions come with teaching and research responsibilities, but often, they do not. But they do offer the opportunity to be deeply involved with the operations of your school and give you the chance to see and make major changes at a larger level.

It is worth noting that sometimes those who go into academics expect one thing and find something else they weren't expecting. Some get into academia to research but neglect their teaching while others focus on the teaching without performing independent research. The quality highly valued in academia is the rare person who can communicate effectively in the classroom and perform innovative and interesting research.

# Chapter 2

# Political Science as a Degree

Why pick political science to major in? Why pick any major when you enter college? Undergraduate degrees are generally designed to do two things: one, give students a general background in the liberal arts and sciences and, two, provide specialized classes in a chosen field to prepare students for a future career or further study. In picking what major to pursue as an undergraduate, then, you are anticipating the type of career and future you would like to pursue. As outlined in Chapter 1, there are myriad career paths open to those who have received degrees in political science, and the classes and activities you choose to engage in can have a significant impact on just how well prepared you could be for that career opportunity. This chapter, then, explores some of the road maps that you can choose to follow right now as an undergraduate student to ensure that you are best positioned for whatever it is you have the desire to pursue.

First, consider what makes political science not only interesting to learn about but valuable for career-minded college students. Under the broad heading of *political science* actually fall at least five major subfields or specialty areas: American politics, comparative politics, international relations, political theory, and public policy and administration. While all have to do with politics, the subfields concern themselves with very different aspects of it. Some undergraduate degree programs will explicitly direct you to choose one or two concentrations or fields in which to focus your classes. However, if you have little to no experience with political science, you may find this difficult to do. For a moment then, let us briefly review what each of these subfields entails.

International relations concerns itself with the study of how countries around the world interact with each other. It is focused on the creation and utilization of theories such as realism, which proposes that states, among other things, are self-interested rational actors seeking power, and liberalism, which believes that anarchy is not a logical outcome of world affairs and that states can and should work together and with international organizations to create legal and ethical norms that guide state behavior. Other theories include constructivism, feminism, and even Marxist conceptions of international relations. International relations scholars also study incidences of war and peace and prescribe policy directions they believe might be the most fruitful.

Comparative politics is an effort at studying patterns of politics and policy around the world. While this sounds similar to international relations, it differs from in it that they are not entirely concerned with how states behave among each other. Instead, comparativists study all aspects of governing, from institutions like legislatures, executives, and judiciaries, to democracy, development, economics, and transitions away from communism. Often, as the name implies, comparative scholars utilize the comparative method in order to understand politics across multiple countries and regions.

American politics is the study of politics in the United States. While we in America consider this a major subfield of political science, from the perspective of other political scientists around the world, American politics is merely comparative politics studied solely in the United States. To an extent, this is true; however, many of the major topics of study in comparative politics are not quite applicable to the United States, either because the phenomena are not taking place in the U.S. (for example, communism or development) or the ideas are uniquely situated in the U.S. (The institutional position of the president was developed in the United States.) In any case, those who study American politics look both at institutions like the Congress and the presidency but also political behavior, the way in which individuals behave politically. Among other things, this includes voting, the media, political parties, interest groups, and political socialization.

Political theory is the original focus of political science, and examinations of it go back to Ancient Greece. In general, political theorists concern themselves with understanding the philosophical underpinnings of government, what makes a government or state good or bad. Enlightenment philosophy expanded on this tradition with an exploration of natural rights and the duties of a government. Political theory is still vitally important today both for our understanding of political processes and the continued search for the "best" government.

Finally, public policy and public administration focus on the development of policy and the administration of it, respectively. Public policy classes cover the basic policy processes and policy analysis, or the scientific means of comparing policy choices and understanding their ramifications. For as many things as the government does, there are different types of policy areas that can be studied, including transportation, education, infrastructure, taxes, and science and technology. Public administration looks at the system of carrying out governmental activities, including an understanding of the bureaucracy and how it operates. Depending on how one looks at these two areas, some will consider them one subfield while others will see them as two.

Even though these different areas of political science all look at politics from a different perspective, there are still commonalities across all political science classes, including what professors ask you to do. These skills and abilities will make you attractive to future employers, and once you can identify them, you can use them to highlight your individual strengths and skills. Think about some of the things your professors will ask you to do:

— Read a moderate to substantial amount of articles, books, and research
— Write analytical, comparative, or argumentative papers
— Work in groups to complete class assignments
— Think on your feet and participate in class discussions
— Conduct your own research and write your own research papers
— Participate in debates
— Learn about statistical methods, how to gather data, and how to analyze it properly

These skills do not benefit you only in the classroom. Large amounts of required reading will sharpen your skills in taking in large amounts of information and processing them. You'll learn how to read for major and important concepts and assimilate them into your own knowledge base. Writing papers allows you to work on your writing skills, along with proper and effective communication. Your ability to communicate effectively with professors and others is a valuable and important skill and perhaps more so as society moves to technological communication methods. Working with others enhances teamwork; although many students will complain about the need to work with others (and thus have their grade depend on others), many situations in the workplace will require such work. Conducting your own independent research will teach you how to determine what information is valid and not, how to bring together multiple streams of information, how to create your own data, and how to evaluate your own information in light of what already exists. Finally, knowledge of statistical methods can contribute to careers in data management and even public opinion.

## Planning Your College Career

As discussed previously, some undergraduate political science programs ask you to choose a concentration while others don't. Even if this is not required, you will want to select your classes based on what will be most valuable in your career field. It would not make much sense, for example, to take a majority of your classes in international relations if you want to pursue a career in a public policy area like education. This is not to suggest that you take no classes in areas other than your concentration or area of interest; indeed, most programs will require you to take at least one class in multiple subfields. Rather, this is to suggest that you be strategic when thinking about the types of classes you choose. Choosing one field now does not foreclose your ability to pursue another sometime in the future.

Further, as many new college students quickly learn, there are many different activities, clubs, and organizations that they can participate in across campus and in their communities. Although many undergraduates choose activities that appeal to them personally, you can also choose to participate in activities that enhance your appeal to future employers. (This is *not* to say that you shouldn't participate in things you *want* to do.) Clubs like College Democrats or College Republicans, teams like speech and debate or Model United Nations, organizations such as student government, and internships in business, politics, or the community are readily available on most college campuses and can give you a taste of what careers in each might be like. Combining the skills, knowledge, and extracurricular activities of a full college career makes for a well-rounded student, citizen, and employee.

The remainder of this chapter will concern itself with providing you with pathways to potential careers. Following the outline of Chapter 1, this chapter will suggest the types of classes and activities that you may want to consider as you prepare yourself for life after college. This does not, by any means, substitute for consultation with a knowledgeable professor or advisor. Your professors and advising team are there as resources to be used by you in planning out your college career and can provide university-specific advice as you consider your options. They can also provide advice relevant to your own personal situation.

One final note is this: The suggested class and activity suggestions here speak only to political science and politics-related extracurriculars. Classes in other fields, such as history, business, math, culture, and language, may also be appropriate depending on your own situation.

## Looking for an Internship

Many schools and universities offer opportunities for internships either in local political offices, in your state capitol, or Washington, D.C. In addition to the work, some often come with academic responsibilities, such as research or a classroom component. In any case, internships offer students an excellent opportunity not only for experience in a field you may be thinking about moving into after graduation but to make connections that will be helpful in the future. If you are looking for dedicated internship programs in Washington, D.C., the following websites will be of interest:

*DCInternships.org:* The Fund for American Studies sponsors several internship programs in and around D.C. and the world.

*Wiidc.org:* The Washington Internship Institute

## Government Jobs

*Elected Officials.* Working for elected officials is quite possible based on one's college career and activities, as many of the things that make your résumé attractive can be done now, while in school. Students wishing to pursue this line of work are best served by classes in American politics, especially in Congress and the presidency. These courses will help you understand how and why each branch works the way it does so that you are not so bewildered once you get there. Classes regarding other actors, such as interest groups and political parties, will also contribute to your ability to work in a competitive congressional environment. Secondary classes, including public policy, statistics, and research methods, will impart skills that will be important in working for politicians whether at home or in Washington, D.C.

In thinking about the types of activities you may wish to engage in, participating in the College Democrats or the College Republicans (depending on your own political persuasion) can help connect you with the local political community. Being involved in student government will also expose you to the community and give you an opportunity to better your college campus. Most importantly, internships with local politicians or in Washington, D.C., itself can get you a foot in the door and an opportunity to display your value to a congressional or political office. If internships are not available at your school, you can offer to volunteer for local elected officials in their offices to give you similar experience, just without the college credit.

*The Military.* Since the job of the U.S. military is to carry out and enforce U.S. foreign policy, a mix of classes in American politics and international relations would be the most appropriate. Those considering a future in the military will want to understand not only the vagaries of American politics and the dynamics of why they will do what they do but also international affairs and how they fit into the broader international picture. Specific class suggestions include the presidency, Congress, U.S. foreign policy, theories of international relations, and war and peace. Secondarily, students may also wish to take classes in comparative politics, especially development and regional politics, including the Middle East, Far East, and Europe.

When it comes to other things you can do to further your career aspirations, participating in the ROTC program is the most direct route from college to the military. Depending on your interests, ROTC programs from the Army, Navy, and Air Force can offer assistance and scholarships, although not all may be available on your college campus. Additionally, opportunities for community leadership and engagement will enhance your emerging leadership skills. Finally, Model United Nations programs will give you a look at the often frustrating world of diplomacy and UN negotiations, which can aid your perspective.

*The Bureaucracy.* As detailed in Chapter 1, there are any number of career paths in the federal bureaucracy to consider. In general, suggested classes would fall in the realm of public policy, public administration, and American politics. Specifically, classes of interest include Congress, the bureaucracy, bureaucratic politics, general public policy, policy analysis, and even policy evaluation. If there is a specific policy area that you wish to pursue, classes focusing specifically on it may be available at your college or university. Additionally, some universities offer public law classes that can assist you in understanding the job of the federal and state bureaucracies.

Internships with local government agencies offer a vital glimpse into the life of a government agency. These internships will give you the opportunity to see what working in such an office might be like, even if it is a state or local bureaucracy. These internships will also allow you to further understand a particular policy area. If internships are unavailable, consider seeking student employment within your university's administration. Student jobs are often plentiful, and while they may be a bit tedious, you can gain an inside understanding of why things happen as they do.

Specifically for the Foreign Service, while there are no explicit educational requirements, the Foreign Service exam tests on areas as diverse as economics and politics to history and culture. Since the job revolves around the function of carrying out U.S. foreign policy, classes in international relations and comparative politics are the most valuable. The Department of State also places immense value on significant international experience, so you should consider participating in study abroad programs or international volunteering activities. Model UN can also be helpful in introducing you to a major international organization and providing valuable training in diplomacy and negotiation.

Similar to the Foreign Service, if you wish to pursue an opportunity with the Peace Corps, knowledge of comparative politics and international relations will be important. In particular, classes on international development, international organizations, and international and comparative political economy would be useful, as you will need to select the projects you wish to apply for. As such, you will need to make yourself an attractive candidate partially based on what knowledge and skills you can bring to that project. Study abroad programs are also useful but so would experience with community volunteering and service. Most colleges offer opportunities to work in the community and service organizations, and fraternities and sororities pursue similar lines of work. Some universities partner with the Peace Corps in the form of Peace Corps Prep, which imparts skills and knowledge to help you make the most of both applying to the Peace Corps and working as a volunteer.

## Lawyers

Those wishing to go to law school often follow similar paths as undergraduates, regardless of whether they want to go into public service or private practice. Political science is one of the most popular choices of undergraduate degree programs for future lawyers precisely because of the classes and skills taught. Future lawyers will want to take classes in American politics, especially classes on the judiciary, judicial process, constitutional law, and other political institutions, including Congress, which makes the laws. Some schools will offer classes in business law or other specific fields that can be good preparation for law school. Additionally, classes in ethics, logic, communication, and advocacy and rhetoric serve as good foundations for law school and excellent preparation for the LSAT.

Colleges and universities provide a number of opportunities for future lawyers to take advantage of before law school. Moot courts and mediation teams expose students to processes that they will likely encounter, if not in law school then certainly while in practice. Speech and debate teams hone communication skills and allow you to practice thinking and arguing on your feet. Often, schools will have prelaw clubs that provide enrichment opportunities to students, including preparation for the LSAT.

## Private Sector Jobs

*Campaigns and Elections.* Working on a political campaign can be quite exciting, fast paced, and interesting. But if you plan on working on American elections, a broad background in American politics will be helpful. This includes classes on political parties, interest groups, Congress, and the presidency. Additionally, many schools offer classes specifically on campaigns and elections, which are highly recommended. Further, because of the media-intensive environment in which campaigns are played out, you may also wish to take classes in the media and communications.

Fortunately, there are also many options for extracurricular activities should you be interested in pursuing these types of jobs. Participating in student government will not only give you an insider's view of the work being done at your school but also an opportunity to try out some campaign techniques and tactics as you work to be elected. Joining College Democrats or Republicans will give you an opportunity to network with like-minded students and be connected to the local political community where you may initially work. Finally, participating in an internship with a campaign or volunteering for one will give you a firsthand look at what is required to run a successful political campaign. These activities, combined with the recommended classes, will create a solid foundation for careers after college.

*Business and Finance.* Since a combination of political science and business will often take you into the realm of international business and finance, general classes in both comparative politics and public policy will be helpful. This includes classes in political economy, which could focus on general concepts and ideas about how politics influences the economy, or comparative political economy, which examines how states around the world become engaged economically. Classes in international and comparative development are also ideal. Finally, within the political science realm, you may wish to take classes in public policy that focus specifically on policy analysis and evaluation. Future employers will find these skills helpful as they implement new programs or policies. If you are interested in combining business with political science, it would also be helpful to pursue classes in business, as either a minor or a double major, if possible.

While it could appear that few other activities actively combine these two elements, many schools offer business or investment clubs that will enhance your business skills, particularly if political science will be your sole major. Additionally,

Model United Nations is also a chance to put these two areas into use, as many of the topics that the UN often confronts have to do with international finance and development.

***Nonprofits, Nongovernmental Organizations, and Foundations.*** At the top of the list of organizations you may want to join after college under this heading might be interest groups or other nongovernmental organizations. As such, classes in interest groups, lobbying, and political behavior are good starting points. Also suggested are classes in public policy, as this would be the area your group might be seeking to change, and campaigns and elections, since these groups are often heavily involved if not in political campaigns then media and awareness campaigns. In a secondary area, classes in organizational leadership will prepare you to work in this field and instill general principles of management and leadership that potential employers will find attractive.

As far as relevant activities and extracurriculars are concerned, there are likely to be a fair number of organizations at your school involved in volunteer and service work. Even if there aren't, actively volunteering for a nonprofit or local charity would be an excellent introduction to the field. For example, the American Cancer Society has local field offices across the United States; volunteering not only gives you an opportunity to make a difference in your community but to become familiar with the activities that groups like the ACS engage in. Finally, if you can find no groups you might be interested in volunteering with, you can always organize your own group or fund-raising activity to heighten community awareness on a topic close to you.

***Think Tanks***. Since think tanks focus more on researching, investigating, and proposing solutions in various policy areas, classes of interest include those in public policy (both process and method along with substantive policy areas that are of interest to you), public administration, and research methods. A study of research methods should include not only basic statistical work but also quite possibly qualitative work, should your school offer additional methodology classes. Since think tanks exist to research and provide advice across the policy spectrum, depending on the area of politics you are interested in, general classes in American politics, comparative politics, or international politics would also be called for.

A fantastic opportunity helpful for future work at a think tank would be working with faculty as a research assistant. In this position, you assist with the faculty member's research all the while learning about research methods and the work that goes into producing reliable findings. If such positions are unavailable at your school, you could request to work on your own research project under the direction of a faculty member who would help guide you through the rigorous research process. Many schools today encourage undergraduate research and offer opportunities for you to show off your work in undergraduate research forums or conferences or even undergraduate research journals.

***Media.*** A profession in political journalism or communications is greatly helped by basic knowledge of the political system, which will not only allow you to understand the comings and goings of the political scene but to communicate that to the press or to the public. As such, classes in institutions such as the presidency or Congress would be helpful, along with courses in political behavior, interest groups, political parties, and even public opinion. Some communications departments even offer courses in political communications and media. It would also serve you well to consider communications classes in either (or both) print or visual media along with writing courses to sharpen your skills at both written and oral forms of communications.

Working with the student newspaper is an excellent opportunity to practice many of these skills, along with gaining an understanding of the inside workings of journalistic endeavors. For example, writing for a newspaper will come with significant limitations on the space you have to report in, enhancing the need for clarity and directness when it comes to your writing. Internships may even be available with larger local newspapers. In thinking about verbal communications, some schools have television or radio channels, giving students an opportunity to learn the behind-the-scenes work, along with creating the content that will be aired. Finally, participating in speech and debate teams will allow you to sharpen your rhetorical skills, forcing you to think on your feet as you rebut the arguments of others, something that you are likely to encounter often in political communications.

*Teaching.* If you are thinking about a career teaching in middle or high school and are majoring in political science, you will want to focus your studies in American politics classes. If you plan to teach in America, these are likely to be the topics that you will be covering, so courses in the presidency, Congress, the judicial system, and even political behavior will prepare you well for relaying those ideas to younger citizens. At a secondary level, you may wish to either minor in or take several classes in education—for example, classroom management, assessment, and teaching methods.

Usually, when a student majors in education, work in a local school is required not only for graduation but certification. If you are taking an alternative route to secondary education, this may not be required of you. Still, you should consider volunteering in a local school, applying to be a substitute teacher (if possible), or serving as a teacher's aide. This will give you an up-close view of what teaching will be like should you wish to pursue such a career. Additionally, participating in activities like Model United Nations or speech and debate can give you the experience necessary to either assist in or run high school programs of a similar nature.

## Academics

The academic career path is an extensive one that could lead to job opportunities in fields other than higher education. When considering such an option at the undergraduate level, you should take as wide a range of classes as possible to expose you to the entire field of political science. This will allow you to make an informed decision at the graduate level of which subfield you would like to pursue the most. Often, the subfield you are most attracted to will change depending on your exposure to it.

Ensuring that you have the best information on which to base a future choice should be paramount at the undergraduate level.

Since pursuing a graduate degree in political science will come with an expectation of independent research, it will be helpful to participate in the types of research experiences that you would consider if you wanted to work in a think tank. This includes becoming a research assistant or working on your own research project under the advisement of a faculty member.

## Conclusion

This chapter has offered the briefest of looks at the career paths that can result from a political science degree, suggesting the types of classes and activities you may want to consider. Again, this is not to discourage you from pursuing other activities while in college; it is those things that you want to do that make you a well-rounded student and citizen. Further, if there are interesting classes to you outside of the political science realm, you should not be discouraged from taking them. It is acceptable to venture outside of your comfort zone to explore other potential options. At the end of the day, college is about discovering your passions and desires that lead to a career.

# Chapter 3

# Acing the Interview

Although entering into a career and searching for a job may seem daunting and impossible, remember that when you started college, completing your degree probably felt the same way. By relying on your own knowledge and skills and the advice of trusted professors and advisors, transitioning from an undergraduate to a professional will soon feel far less intimidating. This chapter provides some ideas and hints not only for looking for a potential employer but in applying and interviewing for a job.

## Looking for a Job

In the age of the Internet, looking for a job is easier than ever. While you might have a specific opening or job type in mind, young job seekers should also keep an open mind about the types of opportunities available. Some may appear to be "beneath you," but in these cases, getting a foot in the door in a lower-level position can be helpful. You may come to understand your employer and their needs better and how you can help them in fulfilling their goals. You can also get a broader handle on the contours and rigors of the job to ensure that that particular line of employment is what you are looking for. Finally, you may become interested in something other than what you originally started out wanting through that initial position. Of course, this does not mean that you shouldn't aim high, just that you should be open minded as you head out of college and into a career.

There are various websites and sources available for young job seekers with a political science degree. If you are looking for a job in the federal government, your first stop should be USAJobs.gov. USA Jobs is the destination for applying for all federal positions other than the Foreign Service. Not only can you search available opportunities, you can and should post your résumé to the site, which will allow agencies to recruit you directly. At the time of this writing, the federal bureaucracy has a program for recent college graduates who have graduated within two years (or six years for military veterans). The recent-graduates program provides a position along with specialized career training that can lead to a permanent position within the bureaucracy. The program allows graduates to transition from college into a career path in government. For information on this and other job opportunities for recent graduates, visit https://www.usajobs.gov/Help/working-in-government/unique-hiring-paths/students.

Additionally, when looking to apply to the federal government, keep in mind that agencies often give priority to certain classes of individuals, including military veterans and their spouses, individuals with disabilities, and minorities. Be sure to highlight any potential hiring advantage you may have on both your résumé and USA Jobs profile.

The only federal employment not listed on USAJobs.gov is that of a Foreign Service officer (FSO). Becoming an FSO is an arduous process, as outlined previously, and includes the completion of the Foreign Service officer test and submission of a personal narrative as initial steps. For further information on this process, as well as instructions on how to register for the test, visit https://careers.state.gov/work/foreign-service/officer.

Once again, working in Congress does not necessarily mean only working for a member of the House or Senate on her or his personal staff. Staffers and assistants are needed to help committees across Capitol Hill and fill the ranks of associated congressional organizations, like the Congressional Budget Office and the Government Accountability Office. The House of Representatives career page can be found at http://www.house.gov/content/jobs and offers information on employment with members and other House offices. The Senate's website is https://www.senate.gov/pagelayout/visiting/h_multi_sections_and_teasers/employment.htm. For careers with the CBO, visit https://www.cbo.gov/about/careers/jobs, and for the GAO, visit http://gao.gov/careers/index.html.

If you wish to work for a state or local government or government agency, the search process can be a bit more convoluted. Most every state has a website like USA Jobs, which can provide information on available job openings and directions for applying. Once again, however, requirements for state employment do vary from state to state. For example, in Oklahoma, you must first apply through their employment website for available openings, and if you meet the basic requirements, you may be asked to complete a merit examination. Florida, on the other hand, does not have a requirement for such a test. No matter the state in which you are applying, be sure to completely understand not just the requirements for the job in which you are interested but what you must complete in order to be considered for it.

## State Government Employment Websites

| | |
|---|---|
| Alabama | https://personnel.alabama.gov |
| Alaska | http://jobs.alaska.gov |
| Arizona | http://www.hr.az.gov/AZStateJobs |
| Arkansas | http://www.arkansas.gov/jobs |
| California | https://jobs.ca.gov |
| Colorado | https://www.colorado.gov/pacific/dhr/jobs |
| Connecticut | das.ct.gov/employment |
| Delaware | http://delawarestatejobs.com |
| Florida | https://jobs.myflorida.com |
| Georgia | http://team.georgia.gov/careers |
| Hawaii | http://dhrd.hawaii.gov/job-seekers |
| Idaho | https://dhr.idaho.gov |
| Illinois | work.illinois.gov |
| Indiana | http://www.in.gov/spd/careers |
| Iowa | https://das.iowa.gov/human-resources/state-employment |
| Kansas | http://admin.ks.gov/services/state-employment-center/sec-home |
| Kentucky | https://careers.ky.gov |
| Louisiana | http://www.civilservice.louisiana.gov |
| Maine | http://www.maine.gov/bhr/state_jobs |
| Maryland | http://www.dbm.maryland.gov/jobseekers/Pages/jobseekersHome.aspx |
| Massachusetts | http://www.mass.gov/portal/employment/finding-a-job |
| Michigan | http://www.michigan.gov/mdcs/0,1607,7-147-6876—-,00.html |
| Minnesota | https://mn.gov/mmb/careers |
| Mississippi | https://www.mspb.ms.gov |
| Missouri | http://www.mo.gov/work/job-seekers |
| Montana | https://statecareers.mt.gov |
| Nebraska | http://statejobs.nebraska.gov |
| Nevada | http://nv.gov/employment |
| New Hampshire | https://das.nh.gov/hr |
| New Jersey | http://www.state.nj.us/nj/employ |
| New Mexico | http://www.spo.state.nm.us |
| New York | https://www.ny.gov/services/employment |
| North Carolina | http://www.nc.gov/jobs |
| North Dakota | https://www.nd.gov/category.htm?id=95 |
| Ohio | http://careers.ohio.gov |
| Oklahoma | https://www.jobaps.com/OK |
| Oregon | http://www.oregon.gov/employ/pages/default.aspx |
| Pennsylvania | http://employment.pa.gov/SitePages/Home.aspx |
| Rhode Island | http://www.apply.ri.gov |

*(Continued)*

(Continued)

| | |
|---|---|
| South Carolina | http://www.admin.sc.gov/humanresources/applicant-information/career-opportunities |
| South Dakota | http://sd.gov/employment.aspx |
| Tennessee | https://www.tn.gov/hr/topic/employment-opportunities |
| Texas | http://www.twc.state.tx.us/jobseekers/job-search |
| Utah | http://statejobs.utah.gov/jobseeker |
| Vermont | http://humanresources.vermont.gov |
| Virginia | http://jobs.virginia.gov |
| Washington | http://careers.wa.gov |
| West Virginia | http://www.personnel.wv.gov/job_seekers/Pages/default.aspx |
| Wisconsin | https://wisc.jobs/public/index.asp |
| Wyoming | http://ai-hrd.wyo.gov/human-resources-division/job-seekers |

If you are considering a career in teaching, again, it is nearly impossible to provide one set of guidelines for how to go about looking for and applying for a position. Once you have decided where you would like to teach, call or visit the website of the school district in which you would like to apply. Additionally, schools can be quite helpful in directing you to appropriate resources. Teach for America, the program where you can volunteer to teach in an underserved school district for two years, requires an online application and interview. If you are interested, you must apply the year before you wish to begin teaching. For more information, visit teachforamerica.org.

Aggregation websites such as GlassDoor.com, Indeed.com, and Monster.com are excellent sources of job opportunities from private businesses, interest groups, think tanks, and related organizations. Like USA Jobs, they also offer you the ability to post your résumé. LobbyingJobs.com also offers listings specific to lobbying and interest groups, but the search results are likely to be far more limited than what you would encounter on these larger sites.

Should you be interested in a job with a specific organization, you can always visit their own website. Some example organizations include the following:

| | |
|---|---|
| – Brookings Institution | https://www.brookings.edu/careers |
| – American Heritage Institute | http://www.heritage.org/about/job-bank |
| – Freedom House | https://freedomhouse.org/content/career-opportunities |
| – RAND Corporation | http://www.rand.org/jobs.html |
| – United Nations | https://careers.un.org/lbw/Home.aspx |
| – World Health Organization | http://www.who.int/employment/vacancies/en |

| | |
|---|---|
| – World Bank | http://web.worldbank.org/external/default/main?pagePK=8453982 |
| – International Red Cross | https://www.icrc.org/en/who-we-are/jobs |
| – CARE International | http://www.care.org/careers |
| – Doctors Without Borders | http://www.doctorswithoutborders.org/work-us-0 |
| – Greenpeace | http://www.greenpeace.org/international/en/about/jobs |
| – American Civil Liberties Union | https://www.aclu.org/careers |
| – National Rifle Association | http://careers.nra.org |
| – PETA | http://www.peta.org/about-peta/work-at-peta/search-jobs-peta |

For academic-related positions, two excellent resources are APSANet.org, the official website of the American Political Science Association, and the Chronicle of Higher Education, at chronicle.com. To access APSA's eJobs listing, you will need to join APSA; however, student rates are available. The APSA job listing is the primary listing of academic political science positions across America. The Chronicle of Higher Education also provides a comprehensive job listing; however, their listings can include most every academic field and not every political science position will appear.

Finally, when looking for a position, the social-media site LinkedIn can also be helpful as a resource. LinkedIn allows you to post your resume and personal profile and "link" with professionals both in and out of your field. While this can be an excellent resource for finding potential employment, keep in mind that ultimately LinkedIn is a social-media site, and you should be careful about what you post on your profile. (See the Social Media box for further information.)

## Preparing an Application

Depending on the field you wish to enter, employers are likely to require different components for an application. To that end, you should read job postings carefully and prepare everything that an employer wants and nothing extraneous. This will put extra pressure on you to ensure that you communicate your potential value in the elements that an organization does request. And although every application will be different, there are several parts that will be held in common that you should have prepared including a résumé, cover letter, letters of recommendation (or names and contact information for personal references), and potentially a portfolio of your past work. This section will outline some of the key fundamentals that go into preparing each of these items.

## Social Media

While most people use some form of social media, whether it is Facebook, Twitter, Snapchat, or Instagram, if you are looking for a job or think you will be looking for a job in the future, you should bring a level of caution to what you are posting. With the Internet today, there is little in the way of privacy or regulating who will see what you are writing and doing. At the end of your time in college, you may come to find things on your social-media feeds that you would not want potential employers seeing or reading. Given this, keep these guidelines in mind:

— Do not post anything that might make a bad impression. If you wouldn't want your parents seeing it, you wouldn't want an employer seeing it either.
— Do not post embarrassing photos or stories.
— Do not post anything inflammatory or controversial.
— Make sure your privacy settings are at the highest level; allow only the people you want to see what you are doing.
— Search for yourself in a search engine and address any search results that may be potentially harmful to your application.
— Whenever you post anything, always assume that *everyone* can see it.

## Résumés

Résumés provide a quick snapshot of your work and educational experience. When preparing your own, you are likely to find multiple templates or examples from which to work; there is no one perfect or standardized version that a résumé should be in. However, in general, your résumé should be clean, succinct, and absent any fancy fonts, images, or styles. These stylistic elements will keep your résumé free from clutter and communicate professional polish to employers.

Excellent résumés will all contain the same sections: a heading with your name and contact information, your career objectives, education, relevant work experience, and other professional experiences. The heading should contain your name, address, phone number, and e-mail address. If you are relying on an e-mail address from your college or university, you should get an outside e-mail address that includes your name, not a nickname. Do not include any social-media accounts; you may consider building a personal *professional* website, and if so, this would be the place to include the Web address. (More on personal websites appears under the heading "Other Application Elements."). See Figure 3.1 for an example résumé.

The next section allows you to lay out, in brief, your own career goals. As with most of the other sections on the résumé, this section should be brief and contain only one or two bullet points, putting a premium on your clarity and succinctness. If you include this section, the challenge is to be specific enough to speak to the

**FIGURE 3.1**
**Sample Résumé**

John Q. Public
123 Main St.
Anywhere, Any State 12345
(555) 555–6789
johnqpublic@email.com
www.johnqpublic.com

**CAREER OBJECTIVES**
— To assist public officials in serving the public and making public policy
— To use my knowledge of education policy to better the educational system

**EDUCATION**
BA, Political Science, University of America, Washington, D.C.
— Graduated May 2017 with university honors
— Minor in Public Policy
— Emphasis on education policy and research methods; proficient in SPSS and Excel

AA, General Studies, College of America, Washington, D.C.
— Graduated December 2014

**WORK EXPERIENCE**
Substitute Teacher, Local School District, Washington, D.C., 2014–Present
— Served as a substitute teacher for high schools, specifically filling in for history and government teachers.
— Worked with local government teachers on a redesigned curriculum focusing on the end-of-course exam.

Internship with Representative Smith, U.S. Congress, Washington, D.C., January–May 2016
— Interned with Representative Smith's main congressional office.
— Responsible for liaising with constituents and legislative assistants.
— Assisted with a streamlining of office systems to respond to constituents 50 percent faster.

**PROFESSIONAL ACTIVITIES**
— President, College Democrats, University of America, 2016–2017
— Volunteer, Education Interest Group, 2016–Present
— Presented "Education: The Role of the Federal Government" at University of America's Undergraduate Research Showcase, December 2016

position or field you are applying to but not so specific that the statement will have to be redone for each successive application. An example of too general a statement might be, "A career that is fulfilling, rewarding, and challenging" while too specific would be "A position with the lobbying department of Lockheed Martin." Instead, something akin to "Assisting organizations with their government relations needs" would be more appropriate.

The first major section of a résumé should concern your educational background. This should be organized by degree, especially if you have multiple degrees. With each degree, list the institution, graduation date, and major; only include your GPA if it was quite high. You should also include any academic honors that you received, such as cum laude or honors designation. A final bullet point should highlight specific skills, certifications, and training that you received. Make sure to include any statistical skills (including software programs you may be familiar with), languages, or professional certifications (for example, a teaching license or certificate).

Work experience follows your education. The key in this section is to include only those positions that are relevant to your application. If, like many college students, you worked part time for a restaurant or retail store, this may not be necessary to include. However, if you completed any internships or did significant volunteer work with a relevant organization, those positions should be included. Like education, each work experience should be written on its own and include where you worked (including actual geographic location), your position, dates of employment, and a brief description of what your job entailed. This is not the place to elaborate on what you were expected to do and how that relates to future employment, but you should have two to three sentences emphasizing and highlighting your accomplishments and skills gained. You may also wish to include important accomplishments or awards from your employer.

Finally, you can add any other activities that may be relevant. This would include any major research papers or projects that you presented, published, or worked with faculty members on. Any volunteer or extracurricular work that may be directly relevant to the job you are seeking should also be included, for example work in student government, the student newspaper, or other collegiate organizations or activities. Some people may also include a list of personal references with their contact information, but this should only be provided upon request, especially if you intend to post your résumé somewhere public, like a website.

In years past, a general recommendation was to keep a résumé to a page in length; this does not necessarily have to be the case. Use as much space as you require to ensure that all of your education, work, and experience are showcased, however, do not include extraneous accomplishments, such as an intramural sports championship. Be relevant and extensive in what you include, but also make it concise and easy to read for a potential employer who may have to sort through hundreds of other résumés.

If you are considering an academic profession, there is a special form of résumé called a curriculum vita, or CV for short. CVs include much of the same information as a typical résumé does but place a greater emphasis on scholarly employment and research activities. Most CVs typically highlight education first and then specific academic positions and experience followed by research. If you are applying for a graduate program in law or political science, a résumé will typically suit your purposes.

## Cover Letters

Cover letters are an important component of most applications but are unfortunately often overlooked by applicants. A cover letter introduces you to a potential employer and highlights the skills and talents that you can bring to a job. It brings attention to important parts of your résumé and gives an employer a sense of who you are. You should pay special attention to this element and tailor each cover letter for every job you are applying to.

**FIGURE 3.2**
**Sample Cover Letter Heading**

## John Q. Public

123 Main St., Anywhere, Any State 12345
(555) 555–6789
johnqpublic@email.com

May 31, 2017

Mrs. Jane Smith, Chief of Staff
Office of U.S. Representative John Doe
456 Public Avenue
Washington, D.C. 56789

Dear Mrs. Smith,

Overall, a cover letter should be professional in nature. This is quite different from the academic tone that you might have used in preparing papers as an undergraduate. Use of the first person is acceptable, as you should be arguing why you are the best person to fill the position you are applying for. Your writing should be clear and succinct, and the letter should be formatted as a proper business letter (see Figure 3.2). Above all, make sure to proofread your letter to ensure that it is grammatically correct. Do not use informal language or text speak. You are trying to make the best first impression you can, and grammatical errors communicate that you are either sloppy in your writing or are not aware of it, ideas that are harmful to your job prospects.

Prior to preparing a cover letter, create a template for your own personal letterhead. This can be done easily through templates already created in word-processing software like Microsoft Word, or you can design your own. In any case, make sure that your letterhead does not distract from the overall purpose of the document. It should be clear and simple and communicate who you are, your address, and your contact information. Once you have completed this, you can print your cover letters on your letterhead.

When you prepare a cover letter, make sure to address it to a specific person. If the job posting gives a point of contact, address it to that person; if not, look to see who might be in charge of the human relations department or even the head of the department you would be working in. Try to avoid addressing the letter to some vague entity. The first paragraph of the cover letter should introduce yourself and inform the addressee as to what position you are applying for and where you found the position posted. Employers are likely to have multiple job openings, so it will be important to specify exactly which one you are interested in. This is also the place to give a brief idea of why you are qualified for the position you are interested in. If you think of this as a personal essay, this sentence will be your thesis statement on which you will elaborate throughout the rest of the letter.

A cover letter should demonstrate to the employer that you have done your research on the position and the organization and how you can benefit them. Identify two to three major points that you can focus the body of your letter on. For example, if you are applying to work with a member of Congress on her or his staff, think about the types of responsibilities you might be given: dealing with constituents, researching and working on policy issues, and perhaps even working with other members and their staffs on different projects. As a political science major, you will be well prepared and versed in research and writing. You may elaborate on these skills and how they can benefit the member as she or he compiles information on different policy issues and comes up with potential legislative solutions. You could emphasize your communications and teamwork skills that will enhance the member's ability to work across the Congress on broad policy issues. Use specific evidence, where possible, to support these arguments. Was there a research project that you worked on that you presented on campus or elsewhere? Did you work through a student organization on a service project that enhanced your community? Bringing to bear specific examples will help support your assertions and give a potential employer a sense of what you bring to the table.

As with any good essay, a conclusion is necessary. Conclude by reiterating your strongest point or qualification for the job; for example, you might say that your previous experience as an intern or volunteer in a member of Congress's office combined with your political science background will allow you to hit the ground running and contribute to the policy goals of the representative. Politely request an interview and that you be considered for the position. Be sure to thank the addressee for his or her attention and note that you are looking forward to hearing back.

Once again, do your best to personalize the cover letter for each job you apply to. If you submit a more generic cover letter, the employer will be likely to think that you are not that interested in the position or do not care enough to speak directly to what his or her job position requires. It may take extra time and effort to complete, but a proper, well-written cover letter enhances your first impression and communicates your interest in the job.

## References and Letters of Recommendation

At some point in the application process, you will be asked to either provide a list of references or a set of letters of recommendation. These are an important element that serve to support the contentions of your cover letter and reiterate the skills and talents that you bring to a position. Do not wait until you are asked for these to begin thinking about who might be willing to serve as a reference. Professors, advisors, and previous employers are all excellent examples of references that you should consider. Do not ask friends or family to serve as references unless the application specifically asks for them; employers will want someone who can be an independent source of information about you. That doesn't mean, however, that you should ask someone to be a reference that you think will give a negative recommendation. Certainly, you should only ask individuals who (1) know you and can speak to your work and accomplishments and (2) are willing to endorse your job application.

When letters of recommendation are called for, be sure to give your references enough notice and plenty of time to complete them. Provide the reference with the name of whom the letter should be addressed to and their address, especially if the letter is to be mailed. (If it should be e-mailed or delivered via an online system, let her or him know that as well.) Always give your reference a due date; you can politely remind her or him to write and send the letter as that date approaches. Finally, you may wish to provide your reference with your résumé and a personal statement that he or she can use in writing the letter. This will allow him or her to reference specific items and provide supporting evidence for your accomplishments and abilities.

## Other Application Elements

While a résumé and a cover letter are the two most important and requested elements of an application, some employers may request additional supporting documentation. These elements include writing or work samples, a portfolio of past work, unofficial transcripts, or personal statements. You do not necessarily need to have these prepared in advance of an application, but you should, at a minimum, identify what you may be able to gather to complete the application process.

Unofficial transcripts may be the easiest of these to obtain and have at the ready; leading up to graduation—but especially after graduation, when the degree you have earned will appear on the transcript—order a copy from your school's registrar. Be aware that there is a difference between official and unofficial transcripts; official transcripts usually must be sent by the school to the employer and have been unopened prior to them arriving. If you request a transcript and then open it, it will be considered unofficial but will often be sufficient for the application process. Once you have this transcript, scan it using a high-quality document scanner, and save it as a PDF. This will allow you to quickly add it to your application packet.

For portfolios or samples of past work and writing, think back to some of the assignments you worked on as an undergraduate. Was there one that best exemplified your writing skills, be it an argumentative brief, position paper, or summary of a policy area? Was there a research paper that was especially good? If you have taken a research methods class, a research paper might have been required of you; this could serve as one of the examples in your portfolio or even as the writing sample itself. As always, for any work you may be considering including, go back over it with an eye toward clarity and writing. Check for grammatical errors and perhaps consider having a professor review it for you.

Personal statements may be one of the most difficult components to think about and include. Some employers may ask for a more specific version of a personal statement, such as a five- or ten-year plan or a statement about your previous work experiences. For a personal statement intended for an application for employment, you should include information on your education, skills, abilities, and talents and how they might contribute to making you an excellent professional in your field. You may also use this to discuss overall career or education goals. As this is a personal statement, you can also use this as an opportunity to discuss your own personality and characteristics to make your application more personal and more memorable. This might include a discussion of a particularly defining event in your life or how you have been personally touched and affected by the field that you want to enter. Do not, in any case, make this a slapdash affair; put some thought and effort into writing a good personal statement to best exemplify you as a unique individual who could be helpful in whatever it is you choose to do.

Much of this discussion has focused on the traditional elements of an application; the preparation of résumés and cover letters is not a new exercise for job seekers. However, given the technology now available, some candidates have taken advantage of it to make themselves more widely known or better publicized. One of the easiest ways to do this is through a personal website. Creating a personal website is easier than ever and does not require an in-depth knowledge of coding or website construction. Instead, sites like Squarespace.com and GoDaddy.com offer tools through which you can build your own website based on templates or other design elements. These websites do require nominal fees, so be sure to research and compare to get the best cost for what you want to do.

To be sure, a personal website, particularly if the intention is to gain employment, is *not* a blog or a deeply personal chronology of your life. Instead, you are using the tools of the Web to put forward a professional face and showcase what you have to offer. Get a Web address based on your name. No personal pictures, Twitter or Facebook feeds, or commentary should be included. Rather, include your resume, a brief biography, and some examples of your work. Make sure to outline the profession that you are seeking, but also keep it broad enough that someone may be able to envision you in a position other than what you most desire. Follow the guidance in the social media box to make sure that potential employers are getting the best information about you, not the information that may make you appear as a less-than-desirable candidate.

## The Interview

Having submitted your application and all of the required documents, the next step is ideally the interview. Since many of the applications you are likely to submit will be via an online system, it is always a good idea to e-mail the point of contact not only to ensure that she or he received all of your materials but also to reinforce yourself as the ideal candidate given your education and experience. Always be polite, but you can remind her or him that you are available for an interview at her or his earliest convenience.

### Proper E-Mail Communication

Today's main form of communication has moved away from pen, paper, and snail mail to electronic communications in the form of e-mails. Unfortunately, many people take e-mail to be an informal means of communicating; they use improper greetings, poor writing, informal language, and text-messaging shorthand. When using e-mail for job interviews and other professional obligations, messages should be written in a formal manner. When writing formal e-mails, especially e-mails in the course of job hunting, you should keep the following guidelines in mind:

— Always include a descriptive subject line. Do not leave it blank or allow "no subject" to be the entry.
— Include a proper greeting, such as "Dear Mr. Smith."
— Do not use informal language or text speak.
— Always use spell check to correct any spelling errors.
— Proofread your e-mails before sending.
— Include a closing along with your name (e.g., "Sincerely").
— Don't use an e-mail address with a nickname or other informal name.
— Do not include anything in e-mail that you would not say to the individual in person. E-mails often remain saved for quite some time.

## Preparation

The key to any successful interview is to be prepared. While you will be ready to discuss your background and experience, you should spend time researching the company or organization, including its mission and the position you are applying to. This demonstrates to the employer that you are interested in them and gives you another opportunity to state how you can be helpful to them as they carry out their operations. Be familiar with who you are interviewing with or might be working under. During the interview, you will be asked if you have any questions, so this is something else that you should be prepared for. Think of some possible questions ahead of time, but do not focus them solely on the material aspects of the job, such as the pay, vacation, and other benefits. Ask about the responsibilities you would be expected to take on, the working environment, and opportunities to improve and enhance the organization's operations. This again demonstrates a sincere interest in working for that potential employer. At the end of the interview, plan on asking the interviewer what the next steps in the hiring process are and when you can expect to hear from him or her. Reiterate that you can provide any additional information as the employer requires it.

Many colleges and universities have career centers that can help you prepare for interviews, including doing a mock interview. If possible, participate in one of these practice sessions to get a feel for what a professional interview might feel like and encompass. You are likely to be asked questions that you haven't thought of, so feeling your way through thinking on your feet will be helpful. The career counselors will also be able to give you feedback on your performance so that you can improve your interviewing skills.

As the interview approaches, think ahead, and plan carefully. You should dress in business clothes, including a suit and tie for gentlemen and a business suit for women. While this dress code may appear limiting and conservative, feel free to show some personality, whether that is in the tie or lapel pin for men or the color of a blouse or scarf for women. Women should always remember to wear pants or a skirt that reaches the knees and that the clothing is not too tight or revealing. Makeup should not be distracting but used to highlight a natural appearance. Similarly, both men and women will not want a distracting hairstyle or color. You may use body fragrance, but it should not be overwhelming.

Another aspect to plan ahead about is transportation to the interview. Make sure you have a reliable means of transportation and a backup if necessary. Plan on arriving early, not merely on time. Consider any possible traffic or road construction as you think about the amount of travel time that will be required.

## At the Interview

Today, interviews are not solely conducted in person but can be done via the phone or even Skype. If you are participating in a phone interview, try to utilize a landline so as to minimize any chance of the phone call being dropped or being affected by a bad connection. Make sure to take it in a quiet place without distraction and without any extraneous noise. If an employer asks for an interview via Skype or Facetime, treat it as you would an in-person interview. Be appropriately groomed and dressed, but also, choose the background you will be appearing against carefully. You do not want anything distracting or that could send a less-than-ideal message. If possible, make sure the background is a solid color and that the lighting in the room is sufficient for your needs. Practice using Skype. Chances are that the feed will freeze, but continue to respond to questions normally; the interviewer will let you know if they missed any of what you said. If you find yourself uncomfortable with seeing either yourself or the other person on Skype, simply place small sticky notes over the faces so as not to be distracted.

Once at the interview, be confident but not overly so; cocky responses may send a message to the employer that you think you are too good for them or that they are beneath you. Employ a firm handshake, and make eye contact. Having done your research about the organization and thought about how you may be of service to them, answer all questions to the best of your ability, but be honest. If you are asked whether you can do something out of your skill set—for example, Web design—tell the interviewer that while you cannot currently perform that task, you are willing to learn. If you are taken on a tour of the facilities, ask questions, and be involved. Active listening is sometimes more important than talking, so use the interview as an opportunity to learn more about the organization. Do not continuously look at your watch or your cell phone; your cell phone should either be off or on silent so as not to interrupt. Support your argument about why you would be an excellent hire with examples of work that you have previously done. Remember to ask your questions throughout the interview but especially at the end. It is acceptable to have a brief list of what you would like to ask, but do not make the list too distracting.

Given that you will be applying for a position that has something to do with your political science degree, politics is likely to come up in conversation. This is a touchy subject not just in your interview but in general; today, much of the population tends to be polarized and partisan. Make a distinction between jobs that are explicitly partisan, such as working for an elected official or partisan polling operation, and those that are not, such as teaching or lobbying. Be comfortable with discussing politics in interviews for political jobs, but do not appear overtly extreme or angry. Even in a political position, you will need to demonstrate that you can work with people from the other side of the aisle, so while it may be acceptable to express an opinion, do not appear close minded either. If you are applying for a nonpolitical job, take it as an opportunity to show that you are aware of political arguments from both the right and the left. If you want to be a lobbyist, you will probably have to meet with both Republicans and Democrats, so an awareness of all sides of an issue will serve you well.

An often overlooked part of the interview is collegiality. Collegiality refers to your ability to get along and work well with others. Since you will be working with other people and as part of a team, those who are considering hiring you must feel comfortable with you professionally. To that end, ask questions that demonstrate you are interested in the other people you would be working with. Don't be overly personal and ask about families, children, and the like, but take the opportunity to show potential employers that they should be comfortable with you personally—not just with your skills and abilities but with you personally.

Once the interview is over, do not post about it on social media. The company and the interviewer may be checking your social media feeds, and you do not want to appear either overconfident or to be gossiping about the interview. The next day, you can send a thank-you e-mail to the interviewer showing appreciation for her or his time and perhaps stating something about the company that you found to be exciting or intriguing. If you have thought of any additional questions based on the interview itself, this would be the place to ask it.

At the end of the day, you're either going to get the job or not. While the position might have been one that you desired, try not to take it personally if you don't get it. There might have been absolutely nothing wrong with your interview or your performance; the company may simply decide to go in another direction. The fact that you got as far as the interview stage demonstrates the organization's belief that you are at least qualified for the job. At the end of the day, you can always consider an interview practice for the next one.

# Chapter 4

# Choosing a Graduate School

Should your political science career path either lead you toward additional schooling or whether it eventually leads you back to it, many who major in political science will find that they want to go on to learn more about their field. Whether it is going to law school or pursuing graduate education in public affairs, public policy, campaigning, or another subfield of political science, understanding the graduate school process is essential. This chapter looks at both law schools and general graduate schools, including hints for choosing a school that is right for you, applying, and funding. Remember, this is just a starting point; your professors, who have all been through this process before, can provide valuable perspective and insight, as well as advice based on your own personal situation.

## Law School

The process to go to law school can seem quite daunting; the LSAT, the applications, and even the potential cost scare many potentially good lawyers away. This does not have to be the case. In this section, I discuss the law school application process, including the LSAT, but the first task is often to think about where you would like to go to law school. The juris doctor (the resulting degree) generally takes three years to complete, with the first year focusing on required courses, such as contracts, torts, criminal law, constitutional law, and legal research and writing. The second and third years allow you to take classes in a variety of areas but will generally ask you to focus on a particular area of law that you might be interested in. Because different law schools offer various areas of concentration, you should consider what area of law you might want to focus on. To give you an idea of how this can vary between law schools, Figure 4.1 lists the different areas of concentration for two different law schools, the University of Florida and the University of Oklahoma. Some schools also offer certificates in different areas of the law to give you further specialization.

**FIGURE 4.1**
**Law School Concentrations for University of Florida and University of Oklahoma**

| University of Florida | University of Oklahoma |
|---|---|
| Business Law | American Indian and Indigenous Peoples Law |
| Civil Litigation/Appellate Practice | Business, Commercial, and Real Estate |
| Commercial/Bankruptcy Law | Constitutional and Public Interest Law |
| Corporate Transactional Practice | Criminal Law and Procedure |
| Criminal Law and Procedure | Family Law |
| Entertainment and Sports Law | General Practitioners |
| Entrepreneurship and Law | Intellectual Property Law |
| Environmental and Land Use Law | International and Comparative Law |
| Family Law | Litigation |
| Intellectual Property | Oil and Gas, Natural Resources and Energy Law |
| International and Comparative Law–Business | Tax Law |
| International and Comparative Law–Human Rights | Estate Planning |
| Public Service and Government Practice | |
| Real Estate Practice–Land Development | |
| Real Estate Practice–Small Transactional Practice | |
| Trusts and Estate Law | |

Once you have considered the area you might like to focus on, do your research. While looking at law schools, don't just focus on what they teach but also location, requirements for practicums and internships, whether summer classes are required, and cost. Don't get distracted by shiny labels of well-known schools like Harvard, Yale, or Stanford. Depending on what you're interested in and what you're willing to pay, these may not be the best options. While much of this information can be found online, visits should also be conducted. This allows you to meet with a counselor who can discuss personalized class and finance options. Many law schools will give you an opportunity to sit in on a class to get a feel for the style of class and professors. Talk to practicing lawyers to get a feel of what to expect and what to look for in a law school. Attend regional law school fairs to be introduced to schools that might not have initially made your list. Finally, when narrowing down your list of potential schools, be sure to include a variety of schools, from the one you would most like to attend to a backup school, as well as a school that may be the most affordable.

As you are considering your law school options, be preparing for the LSAT, the Law School Admissions Test. The LSAT consists of five sections of multiple-choice questions and one writing section, each of which lasts for thirty-five minutes. The test is designed to test reading comprehension, analytical reasoning, and logic. Since you will need to take the test no later than the fall of the year previous to when you wish to attend, planning for the LSAT should be embarked on approximately two years in advance of when you plan to attend. There are numerous preparation sources available both in person in testing centers and online. To find more information on official LSAT preparation materials, visit http://www.lsac.org/jd/lsat/preparing-for-the-lsat.

As you look to the time to complete the LSAT, you should also begin preparing your application. Identify at least three individuals who would be willing to prepare a letter of recommendation for you. Be sure to give them your résumé, and inform them that they will receive an e-mail asking for their letter. Most law schools in North America use a combined law school admissions system available through the Law School Admissions Council (LSAC) at http://www.lsac.org/index. The LSAC system will ask you to use the Credential Assembly Service (CAS) to organize all required materials, including your undergraduate transcripts and letters of recommendation. LSAC also gives you the opportunity to sign up with its Candidate Referral System so that law schools can look at your information to identify who they want to recruit.

Other items that law schools are likely to request through the application process include personal statements and interviews. Both of these give the admissions committee a better idea of who you are as an individual. While most of us are familiar with the personal statement Elle Woods uses in the movie *Legally Blonde*, these interviews and statements will be far more formal, though you should also use the opportunity to inject them with your own personality. Georgetown University's Cawley Career Education Center describes the personal statement as "a written interview during which you get to choose the question. What one thing do you wish the admissions evaluators knew about you?" One possible tack for this assignment might be to write about a particularly important or defining moment in your life. How did that moment influence you? What about it makes you special and unique? Another strategy might be to write about what inspired you to decide to go to law school. Did your experience with the health care industry show you its faults and flaws and push you to specialize in health care policy and law? In any case, the personal statement should not be taken lightly, and you should work with an advisor to hone and perfect your statement. For other dos and don'ts, see the side box on personal statements.

# Personal Statement Dos And Don'ts

## (Courtesy Victoria Turco, Georgetown University)

### DO

- Discuss possible personal statement topics with your prelaw advisor (or someone else) before you invest a lot of time writing.
- Choose a narrow topic. Offer details about a small topic rather than generalities about a broad topic. Focus on a concrete experience and the impact it has had upon you.
- Be yourself. Do not tell law schools what you think they want to hear—tell them the truth.
- Pay special attention to your first paragraph. It should immediately grab a reader's attention. Reviewers are pressed for time and may not read beyond an uninteresting opener.
- Keep it interesting. Write with energy, and use the active voice. You do not have to explain how your experience relates to your desire to attend law school. Tell a story. Paint a vivid picture. The most interesting personal statements create visuals for the reader, which make your personal statement more memorable.
- Keep it simple and brief. Big words do not denote big minds, just big egos. Choose your words with economy and clarity in mind, and remember that your reader has a huge stack of applications to read. A personal statement generally should be two to three double-spaced pages.
- Proofread. Ask several people to proofread your essay. Grammatical or mechanical errors are inexcusable.
- Include information from your background that sets you apart. If your ethnicity, family, religion, socioeconomic background, or similar factors are motivating you to succeed in law school, be sure to highlight them. You can do this in the personal statement itself or in a separate diversity statement. If you are writing a personal statement and a diversity statement, make sure the two essays address different topics.
- Consider your audience. Most admissions evaluators are professors, third-year law students, or admissions professionals not long out of law school. Therefore, you want to come across as an attentive student, interesting classmate, and accomplished person. Again, consider what you most want them to know, beyond the information provided in the rest of your application.
- Read the application carefully. Most law schools allow you to choose a topic, but some will require you to address a specific question. Follow whatever instructions are provided.

### DON'T

- Do not play a role, especially that of a lawyer or judge. And stay away from legal concepts and jargon. You run the risk of misusing them, and even if you use them properly, legal language may make you appear pompous.

- Do not tell your life story in chronological order or merely restate your résumé. Furthermore, resist the urge to tie together all of your life experiences. The essays that try to say too much end up saying nothing at all.
- Do not become a cliché. You may genuinely want to save the world. Maybe your study-abroad experience transformed the way you look at the world. But these topics are overused. Before writing your essay, consider how your story is unique, and highlight your individuality.
- Do not use a personal statement to explain discrepancies in your application. If your academic record is weak in comparison to your LSAT scores or vice versa, address that issue in an addendum. Emphasize the positive in the personal statement.
- Do not offend your reader. Lawyers rarely shy away from controversial topics, but you should think twice before advocating a controversial view. You do not want to appear to be close minded.
- If you are in the bottom of an applicant pool, do not play it safe. You have nothing to lose by making a novel statement.

**Source:** Cawley Career Education Center, "Law School Personal Statement Dos and Don'ts," accessed February 7, 2017, https://careercenter.georgetown.edu/graduate-law-school/law-school-application/law-school-personal-statement-tips.html.

Some law schools now also ask for either in-person or recorded interviews. Many of the interview tips offered in chapter three will apply to this process as well. For some recorded interviews, you will only have a few minutes to prepare your answers before needing to respond to the online prompts, so take time to practice in advance with questions that might potentially be asked. These include questions about your strengths and weaknesses, what you like to do, why you want to go to law school, and why you want to go to their law school in particular.

All of this should be completed no later than the December prior to when you would like to be admitted. Be sure to look at the individual deadlines of the schools you wish to apply to so that you can be sure of meeting their deadlines. Some law schools offer early decision options; these are similar to those found at the undergraduate level. If you wish to apply under that heading to a school, it will be important to get these tasks done even earlier than the December guidance.

## Graduate School

If studying political science as an undergraduate has stoked your interest in learning more, you may be contemplating graduate school. It is through this specialized education that you can further study those areas which have piqued your interest. Many of the questions noted earlier in terms of location, school, and cost should also be taken into consideration when thinking about where to further your political science education. Much of this also depends on which degree you wish to attain; pursuing a master's can take between a year and a half to three years, and a PhD will typically take upwards of five years. You can obtain a master's degree in political science or another related field like public health, public administration, or campaigning. You could even decide to take graduate classes part time and work a full-time job, in which case, when classes are offered, evening or daytime, may affect your calculus. To this end, consider the following questions as you begin to think about graduate school.

— *What do I want to study?* And more importantly, why do I want to study it? Do I want to become an academic political scientist and teach college, research, and write? Or do I want a more focused graduate education, perhaps in the areas of public policy, public health, or campaigns and elections?
— *If I'm considering an academic career, do I want to begin with a master's degree and then continue onto the PhD?* Doing so would allow me to get my feet wet and better understand what is required in graduate school, but getting a master's first is not a necessary and required first step.
— *Do I plan to work full time and go to school part time?* If so, I will need online and/or evening classes to better fit with my schedule.
— *If I am going to work, what schools will be around me?* What kinds of degree programs do they offer?
— *If school location does not matter, consider what specifically you want to study.* What do you find interesting? What grabs your attention?

Know what you are getting yourself into with graduate work. If you are pursuing a master's degree, know that some make you choose between a thesis track and a qualifying examination track. The difference between these two requirements is that on the thesis track, you will be required to complete an independent research project of your choosing under the guidance of a faculty committee. The examination track will require you to take a series of formal exams toward the end of your classes; the form, substance, and length of time of the tests are all dependent on the school and the faculty members involved. Still other schools will require both of their master's students. (Both qualifying exams and a dissertation are required for most, if not all, PhD programs.) If you have a strong preference about which one of these options you prefer, keep that in mind as you consider where to attend.

Many master's programs (and even some PhD programs) offer concentrated fields of study that you may find interesting. These include public affairs, elections and campaigns, public health, education policy, environmental and conservation work, and public administration. In this way, you can use your political science background to become more specialized and appear more attractive to desired employers. Be sure that you not only know the options that the schools you are interested in offer but that you also consider them; you do not, by any means, have to take a general political science graduate education if that is not what you are truly interested in pursuing.

The answers to these questions should guide you in your search for schools. If you are planning to go a more traditional route in the sense that you want to study political science for academic reasons, one of the biggest criteria that you should consider as you search for schools is the faculty. Compared with the undergraduate level, graduate education has a greater emphasis on faculty–student interaction; if there is a particular aspect of political science—for example, development economics and policy or modern political theory—that you want to focus on, look for schools that have faculty with similar interests. This will ensure not only that the classes you most want will be offered but also that you will have a faculty member who can mentor and guide you throughout the process.

As you begin to narrow down your search, you should begin preparing your application materials. You will require many of the same documents discussed previously, including your transcript, personal statement, recommendation letters, and résumé. Instead of completing the LSAT, however, those looking to enter graduate school will usually need to complete the Graduate Record Examination, or GRE. The GRE has three main sections: verbal reasoning, quantitative reasoning, and writing. Like the SAT or ACT that you took in high school, the purpose of the GRE is to gauge how well you perform at tasks that you will encounter as you move through graduate education. There are numerous online and in-person test preparation resources that you can acquire to help you prepare for the exam. When you are ready to take it, you will need to register for it and take it at an approved testing center. Plan on having taken the GRE at least once the fall before you plan on entering graduate school so that if necessary, you can take it again.

Unlike the law school application process, each school has its own application system and requirements that you will need to take note of and adhere to. Be sure that the people you have identified as writers for your letters of recommendation have sufficient time to complete them and that you have given them a résumé that they can refer to as they write. You should also prepare a personal statement that will introduce you as an individual to the graduate admissions committee. Like the law school personal statement, this should convey your interest in political science, why you wish to attend graduate school, and what you can bring to a program. Plan on completing all of the elements of an application by the December prior to when you wish to begin—or earlier, depending on application deadlines.

As decisions from schools begin to come in and you consider which school to attend, one major item to take into consideration is that of financing. Most graduate schools and programs offer various forms of financial assistance, from fellowships and scholarships to assistantships that require you to work up to twenty hours a week. To be fully considered for one of these funding opportunities, schools will ask that you have all of your application materials in by the deadline; contact those schools to which you have applied to make sure they have received everything, including test scores. It is perfectly acceptable to compare financial packages that are offered and to even negotiate with schools to see if they can improve on other offerings. Graduate classes are more expensive than undergraduate classes, so if cost is a major factor in your decision, pursue the best financial package that you believe you can get.

Once again, the best resource you have in thinking about, planning for, and applying to graduate school is your professors. Not only have your professors been through the process before, but they can guide you to and away from programs based on what you want to study and do with your degree. Seek out their advice and thoughts, and you will be far better prepared for what is ahead.

# Index

Academic jobs, in political science, 12–14
  college career planning and, 23–24
Administrative law, 6
Administrative Procedures Act, 6
American politics, 16
Application (job), preparing an, 29–37
  cover letters, 33–35
  letters of recommendation, 35
  résumés, 30–33

Bureaucracy
  careers in, 4–5
  college career planning and, 19–20
Business and finance
  college career planning and, 21–22
  private-sector jobs and, 8

Campaign finance law, 8
Campaigns
  college career planning and, 21
  private-sector jobs and, 7–8
Careers. See College career planning;
  Political science careers
Center for American Progress, 10
College career planning, 17–24
  academic jobs and, 23–24
  government jobs and, 19–20
  lawyers and, 20–21
  private-sector jobs and, 21–23
Collegiality, 39–40
Comparative politics, 16
Congressional Budget Office (CBO), 2
Cover letters, 33–35
Credential Assembly Service (CAS), 43
Curriculum vita (CV), 33

Degree. See Political science degree

Elected officials
  college career planning and, 19
  working for, 2–3
Elections
  college career planning and, 21
  private-sector jobs and, 7–8
E-mail communication, proper, 37 (box)
Erickson, Erick, 11

Foreign Service officer (FSO), 26
Foundations
  college career planning and, 22
  private-sector jobs and, 9–10

Government Accountability
  Office (GAO), 2
Government jobs, in political science, 1–6
  bureaucracy, 4–5, 19–20
  college career planning and, 19–20
  elected officials, working for, 2–3, 19
  lawyers, 6, 20–21
  military, 3–4, 19
  peace corps, 5
Graduate Record Examination (GRE), 47
Graduate school, 41, 45–48. See also Law
  school

Heritage Foundation, 10
Huffington, Arianna, 11
Huffington Post, 11

Interest groups, 9
International relations, 16
Internship, looking for an, 18 (box)
Interview, the, 25–40
  at the, 38–40
  preparation for, 38

See also Application (job), preparing an; Job, looking for a

Job, looking for a, 25–29
  social media and, 30 (box)

Kennedy, John F., 5

Law school, 41–45. See also Graduate school
Law School Admissions
    Council (LSAC), 43
Law School Admissions Test (LSAT), 43
Lawyers
  college career planning and, 20–21
  government jobs and, 6
  private-sector jobs and, 6–7
Letters of recommendation, 35
LinkedIn, 29

Media
  college career planning and, 22–23
  private-sector jobs and, 10–11
Military
  careers in, 3–4
  college career planning and, 19

Nongovernmental organizations
  college career planning and, 22
  private-sector jobs and, 9–10
Nonprofits
  college career planning and, 22
  private-sector jobs and, 9–10

Office of Management and Budget, 3

Peace Corps, 5
Personal statement, dos and don'ts,
    44–45 (box)
Personal website, 36–37
Political science. See Graduate school;
    Interview, the; Political science careers;
    Political science degree
Political science careers, 1–14
  academic jobs, 12–14
  government jobs, 1–6
  private-sector jobs, 6–12
Political science degree, 15–24
  academic jobs and, 23–24

college career planning and, 17–24
  government jobs and, 19–20
  lawyers and, 20–21
  private-sector jobs and, 21–23
  subfields (major), 15
Political theory, 16
Private-sector jobs, in political science, 6–12
  business and finance, 8, 21–22
  campaigns and elections, 7–8, 21
  college career planning and, 21–23
  lawyers, 6–7, 20–21
  media, 10–11, 22–23
  nonprofits, nongovernmental
      organizations, and foundations,
      9–10, 22
  teaching, 11–12, 23
  think tanks, 10, 22
Public administration, 17
Public policy, 16–17

References, 35
Résumés, 30–33

Social media, 30 (box)
State government employment
    websites, 27–28 (box)
Statement (personal), dos and don'ts,
    44–45 (box)

Teach for America, 28
Teaching
  college career planning and, 23
  private-sector jobs and, 11–12
Think tanks
  college career planning and, 22
  private-sector jobs and, 10
Transcripts, 36
Turco, Victoria, 44

USA Jobs, 4, 26

von Clausewitz, Carl, 3

Websites
  job search and, 26–29
  personal, 36–37
  state government employment,
      27–28 (box)

# About the Author

Wendy N. Whitman Cobb received a BA and MA in political science from the University of Central Florida. She then received a PhD in political science from the University of Florida, where she focused her research on the interaction of institutions with public policy. In addition to the books *Unbroken Government: Success and Failure in Policymaking* (2013) and *The Politics of Cancer: Malignant Indifference* (2017), she has published research in *Congress and the Presidency*, *Space Policy*, and the *Journal of Political Science Education*. Whitman Cobb is an assistant professor of political science at Cameron University, Lawton, Oklahoma.